JUNGLE HIDEAWAYS

ANIMAL FAMILIES

Written by A.J. Wood
Illustrated by Helen Ward

PRICE STERN SLOAN
Los Angeles

Who are playing with their parents?

The playful tiger cubs

Who leads his family through the forest?

Who carries her baby through the branches?

The careful sloth

Who cheep for food on the branch?

The baby birds

Who carries her baby in a pouch?

The tree kangaroo

Who protects his family from danger?

The bull elephant

Who are learning to fly?

The fluffy owlets

Who clings to his mother's back?

The baby lemur

And here is the dormouse family, hiding in their nest.

How many babies can you see?